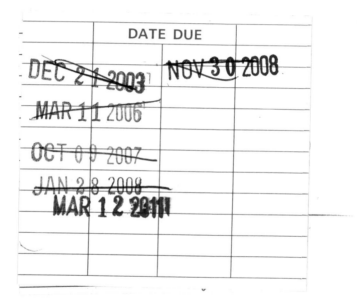

WALKING FOR FREEDOM

THE MONTGOMERY BUS BOYCOTT

WALKING FOR
FREEDOM
THE MONTGOMERY BUS BOYCOTT

BY RICHARD KELSO

Alex Haley, General Editor

Illustrations by Michael Newton

RSVP
RAINTREE
STECK-VAUGHN
P U B L I S H E R S
The Steck-Vaughn Company

Austin, Texas

Published by Steck-Vaughn Company.

Text, illustrations, and cover art copyright © 1993 by Dialogue Systems, Inc., 627 Broadway, New York, New York 10012.

Cover art by Brian Pinkney

Printed in the United States of America
1 2 3 4 5 6 7 8 9 0 R 98 97 96 95 94 93 92

Library of Congress Cataloging-in-Publication Data
Kelso, Richard, 1942–
    Walking for freedom: the Montgomery bus boycott / Richard Kelso; illustrator, Michael Newton.
        p. cm.—(Stories of America)
    Summary: Recounts how the black community of Montgomery, Alabama organized and participated in the 1955 bus boycott which ended segregation on public buses.
    ISBN 0-8114-7218-3,— ISBN 0-8114-8058-5 (softcover)
    1. Montgomery (Ala.)—Race relations—Juvenile literature.
2. Segregation in transportation—Alabama—Montgomery—History—20th century—Juvenile literature. 3. Afro-Americans—Civil rights—Alabama—Montgomery—History—20th century—Juvenile literature.
[1. Montgomery (Ala.)—Race relations. 2. Segregation in transportation—History. 3. Afro-Americans—Civil rights—History.] I. Newton, Michael, ill. II. Title. III. Series.
F334.M79N45 1993
305.896'073076147—dc20   92-18080
                                                                        CIP
                                                                        AC
ISBN 0-8114-7218-3 (Hardcover)
ISBN 0-8114-8058-5 (Softcover)

*This book is dedicated
to those who began the struggle,
and to those who have continued it.*

Introduction
by Alex Haley, General Editor

Sit down. Stand up. No one likes to be told what to do. *Move over there. Come here.* Commands have a way of stinging like bees. Sometimes their stings are poisonous. *Whites only. Get out of that seat.* Segregation was a poisoned command. It was a set of laws and customs that kept black people and white people apart.

But not just apart. Segregation gave white people the best schools. It gave them the best parks and libraries. It gave them the best seats on a bus or a train. It gave black people nothing. Instead it threatened them with jail or violence whenever a command was questioned.

The story you are about to read is about what happens when a community of people say, "Enough." Enough unfairness. Enough segregation. Enough and no more. It's a story of how a community's courage and determination can rob the bee of its sting.

Contents

◆◆◆

1

◆◆◆

No Way to
Start a Vacation

A chilly winter wind was howling around
Mrs. Jo Ann Robinson's car. It was the day
before Christmas 1949, in Montgomery,
Alabama. Mrs. Robinson was driving back
from the Montgomery airport. She had just
dropped off her bags and packages at the airport for her trip home to Cleveland, Ohio.
She didn't want to leave her car out in the
open parking lot while she was away, so she
was driving back to her house to park it in
her garage.

She arrived home and listened to just a
few more seconds of Christmas music before

turning off the car. Then she locked the car in the garage and walked to the bus stop near her house. She planned to take the bus to a friend's house. Then she and her friend would drive to the airport and take a plane home to Cleveland.

The cold wind nipped at her face and legs as she waited for the bus. But she didn't mind it. She was happily thinking ahead to the wonderful Christmas vacation she was going to have.

Soon a yellow bus came chugging along and stopped. She got on without even thinking about it. Her mind was full of vacation thoughts. She dropped her fare in the box. Then she took an empty seat just a few rows from the front. She hardly noticed the two other passengers on the bus. One was a white woman who sat ahead of her in the third row. The other was a black woman who sat near the back.

As the bus began to go, Mrs. Robinson gazed out of the window. A pretty smile came to her light-brown face as she thought about her family and friends in Cleveland. She was eager to see them. She wanted to tell them all about her first four months of teaching at a black college in Montgomery.

Time seemed to disappear as Mrs. Robinson imagined talking to her family and friends. But after a few moments, she thought she heard an angry voice poking its way into her happy thoughts. At first she didn't pay any attention. She was still smiling to herself, and her thoughts were far away.

Then she heard the voice again. It was closer and angrier this time. She turned her head, and there, standing next to her, was the bus driver, his face twisted into a scowl.

"Get up from there!" the driver yelled at her. She hadn't even noticed that he'd stopped the bus and stomped back to her seat. "Get up from there!" he yelled again. His right hand was raised as if he were about to hit her.

Mrs. Robinson was a quiet, thoughtful person. She was polite, and she expected others to be polite to her. The driver's behavior

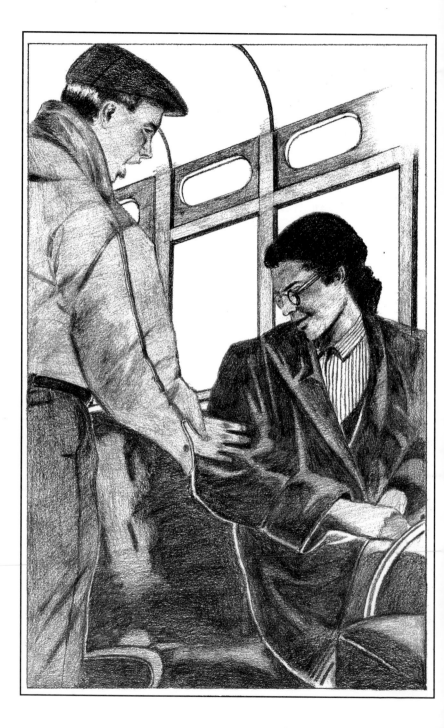

upset and frightened her. She didn't know why he was yelling at her, but she was shocked and too afraid to ask. She surely didn't want to be hit by this big man. She darted out of her seat and ran to the door, tears falling from her eyes.

Full of shame and hurt, she scrambled off the bus. "I felt like a dog," she said later. She was glad none of her students were there to see what happened.

Suddenly, she realized what had made the driver yell at her. She'd sat in one of the rows of "whites only" seats.

In those days in Montgomery, a city law said that seats on the buses were segregated. That meant seats in the front part of the bus were only for white people. Black people had to sit in the back part of the bus. If there weren't enough seats for whites, blacks had to give up their seats.

The law pretended to be "fair." It said that blacks could only be asked to give up their seats *if* there were empty seats in the back.

But in practice this wasn't true. Even if it meant black people had to stand, they were made to give up their seats. Even if there were *no* white passengers at all, blacks could not sit in the first five rows of seats on a bus.

Some of the white bus drivers made the law seem even worse. They yelled at black passengers and called them names. After black passengers had paid their fares, drivers would sometimes order them to get back off the bus and walk to the backdoor to board. The worst of the drivers might then drive off before the black passengers could get back on the bus.

Mrs. Robinson had lived in Montgomery only a short time. Usually she didn't ride the city buses because she had a car. She had been told about the segregated seating law. But it was the furthest thing from her mind when she took a seat on the bus that day.

Still, the bus driver had no right to mistreat her just because she'd forgotten about a law that made no sense. Her shame and fear turned to anger. During her vacation, she kept thinking about how unfair and cruel the driver had been. She wanted to do something about it.

When she got back to Montgomery, she met with members of the Women's Political Council. Most of the women in this group were professionals. They were teachers, nurses, school principals, and social workers. Like many other black community groups in Montgomery, they were trying to improve the way blacks lived in their city. They worked to fight crime, to educate people, and to get people to vote.

Mrs. Robinson told the group about what had happened to her. Then she listened as others told their stories.

"Oh, worse things than that have happened to me," said one woman. "Drivers have called me names I can't repeat here," the woman recalled.

"A driver refused to make change for me, but he made change for white people," another woman reported. "He wouldn't let me on the bus."

"You know, the drivers are just as mean to black men. If we or the men stand up to the drivers, they'll call the police and have us arrested," said another teacher. "Then we might lose our jobs," she added.

Mrs. Robinson realized that what had happened to her had happened to many people. This did not make her any happier, though.

A few months later, in 1950, Mrs. Robinson became the president of the Women's Political Council. Right away she called the mayor of Montgomery, Mr. Gayle. "We would like to meet with you and other city officials," she said. "We'd like to work together with you to solve some problems that black people face when riding the buses."

The mayor invited Mrs. Robinson and a few other women to City Hall. He was friendly. He listened to Mrs. Robinson and other women from the council. But he did not order any changes in the bus law, and he didn't change the way the drivers behaved toward black people.

2

♦♦♦

Enough Is Enough

Year after year went by. The Women's Political Council kept getting reports from blacks about bad treatment on the Montgomery buses. They complained to the mayor, but he refused to do anything about it.

Many black people were getting fed up with the buses and drivers. Some men chose to walk to work rather than take the bus. But most people kept on riding. They believed it was too dangerous to fight back. They were afraid that they would lose their jobs because most of them worked for white people. If they pushed too hard for change, they might even be killed.

In May of 1954, however, the Women's Political Council had had enough. It had been more than five years since Mrs. Robinson had first met with the council. They had been patient too long.

The mayor announced that the bus fares were being raised. Blacks in Montgomery were angry. They didn't mind paying more to ride the buses. But they *did* mind paying more when they were treated unfairly by the law and poorly by the drivers.

On May 21, Mrs. Robinson wrote a letter to Mayor Gayle. She and the Women's Political Council demanded changes in the bus system. They wanted the drivers to stop ordering blacks to board at the back of the bus after they'd already paid at the front. They wanted buses to stop at every corner in black neighborhoods, just as they did in white neighborhoods.

Mrs. Robinson reminded Mayor Gayle that many more blacks than whites rode the buses. She warned him that changes had better be made. Otherwise, blacks would stop riding the buses. They would boycott the buses! Then the buses would lose money.

Mayor Gayle did not answer Mrs. Robinson's letter. So the black community prepared to carry out the council's plan. It took more than a year to get ready. Nearly seventy community groups had to be told about the plan. Church groups, business groups, and social groups all talked about the plan. Some groups were still afraid of causing "trouble" by boycotting the buses. But they all agreed that something had to be done. Finally, the leaders of most of the groups agreed on the idea of a boycott. All they needed was the right moment.

That moment came on the afternoon of December 1, 1955. Mrs. Rosa Parks got on a bus in downtown Montgomery. She was tired from her busy job of sewing clothes at a department store. She got on the Cleveland Avenue bus and sat down in the black section near the back.

The bus rumbled from stop to stop. More and more people got on. Some were white, some were black. Soon there were no more seats in the black section. Many blacks were standing. The white section filled up, too. Then a white man got on and couldn't find a seat.

The driver, James Blake, shouted to the back of the bus. He told Mrs. Parks and three other black people to get up so that the white man could sit down. Blacks weren't even allowed to sit next to whites on a bus. To make "room" for one white rider, four seated black riders were being ordered to move. Mrs. Parks and the other black riders said nothing. And they didn't move.

"Y'all better make it light on yourself and let me have those seats," Mr. Blake warned. The two black people sitting across from Mrs. Parks slowly but surely got up. They didn't want to get up. They knew it was unfair. But they got up anyway. So did the man sitting next to Mrs. Parks. But Mrs. Parks kept her seat.

Mr. Blake looked at Mrs. Parks in the rear-view mirror. "Are you going to stand up?" he asked, raising his voice.

"No, I'm not," Mrs. Parks said firmly.

Mr. Blake stopped the bus and came back to where Mrs. Parks was sitting. He put his hands on his hips and gave her a mean look. "Well, if you don't stand up, I'm going to call the police and have you arrested."

Mrs. Parks was a gentle, quiet woman. But she was also proud and strong. She looked squarely at Mr. Blake and said simply, "You may do that."

Mr. Blake marched off the bus and returned with two policemen. One of the policemen folded his arms and looked at Mrs. Parks. "Did the driver ask you to get up?" he asked.

"Yes," said Mrs. Parks calmly. Her voice showed she was not afraid.

The policeman leaned forward and frowned. "Why don't you stand up?" he asked, getting angry.

Now it was Mrs. Parks's turn to frown. She looked at the three men. Her eyes showed her anger. "Why do you push us around?" she demanded.

"I don't know," said the policeman. "But the law is the law and you're under arrest."

The policemen took Mrs. Parks to jail. They took her fingerprints as if she was a criminal. She *had* broken the law, but the law was unfair. It was based on the idea that black people were not as good as white people. This idea was very different from one of America's most important ideas—that all people are created equal.

Mrs. Parks called home. She spoke to her mother. "Please tell my husband to come and get me out of jail," she said in a tired, angry voice. Mr. Parks was not at home, so Mrs. Parks's mother called Mr. E. D. Nixon.

Mr. Nixon was an important leader in the black community. A tall, dark-skinned man, he worked as a porter for the railroad. And he worked hard to make life better for black people in Montgomery.

When he heard that Mrs. Parks had been arrested, he got busy. He called the jail to find out why she'd been arrested. But the jailer would not tell him. So he called his friend, Clifford Durr, a white lawyer.

Together, Mr. Nixon and Mr. Durr got Mrs. Parks released from jail. Mr. Nixon paid a bond that allowed Mrs. Parks to leave. He would get the money back when she came before a judge to be tried for breaking the bus law.

Mr. Nixon believed the law was unfair, too. He wanted to put a stop to it. As he talked to Mrs. Parks, he had an idea. In Washington, D.C., the Supreme Court had just made a ruling. The ruling said that segregated schools were no longer legal. That meant black and white children could no longer be sent to separate schools. All states had to obey this ruling. If segregated schools aren't legal anymore, Mr. Nixon thought, maybe segregated buses aren't either.

"I think we can break down segregation

POLICE FORM

NAME: Rosa Parks

VIOLATION: Occupation of a passenger seat in an area restricted for caucasians only.

Thumb   1st Finger   2nd Finger   3rd Finger   4th Finger

on the bus with your case," Mr. Nixon told Mrs. Parks.

It was a hard decision for Mrs. Parks to make. If she stood up to the segregation law, bad things might happen to her. She might lose her job. She might be thrown in jail again. She might be hurt or even killed. She wanted to talk to her husband about it.

Mr. Parks was very upset. He knew all the dangers his wife would face. She had already been arrested just for refusing to give up her seat to a white man. By carrying the protest further, his wife would be asking for serious trouble. "The white folks will kill you, Rosa," he said. He wanted her to let the matter drop.

But Mrs. Parks was very brave. She wanted to do something to help the black people of Montgomery. She wanted to make the city a better place for everyone. "I'll go along with you, Mr. Nixon," she said.

Mr. Nixon and other black leaders began making plans. They were going to show that Mrs. Parks should not have been arrested.

They were going to show that Montgomery's black citizens weren't going to accept the bus law anymore. They were going to show that black people were tired of being treated unfairly.

3

Getting Ready to Boycott

Mrs. Robinson knew what to do. As soon as she heard about Mrs. Parks, she called the Women's Political Council. She told them what had happened. They all agreed that this was the moment they had been waiting for. It was time to boycott the Montgomery buses. Mr. Nixon and other leaders liked the idea, too.

Mrs. Robinson got busy quickly. The very evening of the day Mrs. Parks was arrested, Mrs. Robinson went to her college. She wrote a leaflet telling people about the boycott.

"If we do not do something to stop these

arrests, they will continue," she wrote. "We are asking every Negro to stay off the buses Monday in protest of the arrest and trial. Don't ride the buses to work, to town, to school, or anywhere on Monday."

She stayed up all night making thousands of copies of the leaflet. The next morning, students helped her take the leaflets to black homes and businesses all over Montgomery. By Friday afternoon, December 2, many black people knew about the boycott.

Mr. Nixon was busy, too. He phoned the community leaders and the ministers of the black churches. "We need to plan how we'll carry out the boycott," he told them. He asked them to meet at the Dexter Avenue Baptist Church that evening.

Mr. Nixon also wanted to make sure that everybody knew about the boycott. He was even willing to risk letting whites know about it. So he called Joe Azbell, editor of the Montgomery *Advertiser*. "I've got a big story for you and I want you to meet me," he said.

Mr. Azbell met him at the railroad station. Wearing a porter's jacket and black cap, Mr. Nixon showed the editor one of Mrs. Robinson's leaflets. "We're gonna boycott these buses," he said. "We're tired of them fooling with our women—they done it for the last time." Nixon's voice was angry and sharp. But he wasn't mad at Mr. Azbell. He was mad at the Montgomery law, the bus drivers, and the mayor.

"You gonna put this on the front page?" he asked the editor.

"Yeah, I'm gonna try to," Mr. Azbell replied.

Pleased with his meeting, Mr. Nixon waved goodbye to Mr. Azbell. A front-page news story would make sure everyone knew about the boycott. Then he got on a train headed for Atlanta, Georgia. He had to work that night and would not be able to go to the meeting at the Dexter Avenue Baptist Church.

Meanwhile, at the college, Mrs. Robinson

got a note from her boss, Dr. Trenholm. He wanted to see her right away. When she entered his office, she saw that he was angry. His lips were pressed tightly together, and his eyes were squinting. He looked at Mrs. Robinson. Then he held up one of the leaflets she'd written.

"What is this all about?" he asked sharply. "And what do you have to do with it?"

Mrs. Robinson was surprised and a little frightened. She stammered a little and explained what had happened to Mrs. Parks. "Other people have been arrested in the past. All they did was refuse to give up their seats to a white person," she said.

"Were there other seats?" Dr. Trenholm snapped. He knew that the law said that a black person had to give the seat to a white person *only* if there were an empty seat in the black section of the bus.

"No, there wasn't an empty seat," Mrs. Robinson said. Dr. Trenholm was still frowning. He walked back and forth looking down at the floor. But Mrs. Robinson could tell he was thinking carefully.

"Sit down and tell me about this," he said quickly.

Mrs. Robinson sat slowly. She was afraid Dr. Trenholm would fire her. After all, she had used the college's paper and copier. Whites would be angry if they found out. They might say the black college was stirring up trouble. Then the college would be in trouble!

But she also believed she had done the right thing. She took a deep breath to calm herself. Suddenly she didn't care if she was fired or not.

She told Dr. Trenholm about the Women's Political Council and the work they were doing. "We would never do anything that would get the college in trouble," she assured him. "But somebody has to do something," she said boldly.

Finally, she thought she'd said enough. She sighed and looked down at the floor. She wasn't sure what would happen next.

Dr. Trenholm was silent for a long time. Mrs. Robinson could tell that he was changing his mind. She looked at him sitting at his desk. His frown was gone. His face was now long and sad. He put his elbows on his desk and leaned forward. "Your group must continue to press for civil rights," he said. "But you have to be careful," he warned. He seemed tired. "You can't involve the college in this," he said, shaking his head.

Mrs. Robinson was relieved. As she turned to leave, Dr. Trenholm called her back. "You used college paper to run off these leaflets?" he asked.

"That's correct," she said. "The Women's Political Council owes the college for 17,500 sheets of paper. We will pay the bill immediately, sir." But the council didn't pay the bill. It had no money. Mrs. Robinson paid the bill with her own money.

That night more than fifty ministers and leaders met at the church on Dexter Avenue. Besides the ministers, there were also teachers, doctors, lawyers, businessmen, and postal workers. Mrs. Robinson was there, too. Mr. Nixon had done a good job of getting everyone together.

The group made plans for the boycott. They formed themselves into several committees. Each small group had a job to do.

One committee set up a carpool. People with private cars would pick up passengers and take them to work, school, shopping, or elsewhere. The committee decided where the passengers should gather in order to be picked up. They also decided on which streets the cars would travel. That way, everybody would know where to get a ride.

Another committee got in touch with the black taxi drivers in Montgomery. The drivers agreed to take passengers for the same fare the passengers paid on the buses—ten cents.

Everyone agreed that there should be a big meeting Monday night after the day-long boycott. At that meeting they would decide whether or not to continue the boycott.

"We need to let everyone know about that meeting," one leader said. One of the ministers agreed to help write a new leaflet. He was Dr. Martin Luther King, Jr., a newcomer to Montgomery. At age 26, he was younger than most of the other leaders and ministers in the black community. Here's what Dr. King and his committee wrote:

Don't ride the bus to work, to town, to school, or any place Monday, December 5.

Another Negro woman has been arrested and put in jail because she refused to give up her bus seat.

Don't ride the buses to work, to town, to school, or anywhere on Monday. If you work, take a cab, or share a ride, or walk.

Come to a mass meeting, Monday at 7:00 P.M., at the Holt Street Baptist Church for further instruction.

Dr. King and another minister, Ralph

Abernathy, worked until midnight. They made thousands of copies of the leaflet, just as Mrs. Robinson had done. The next morning, Dr. King and Mr. Abernathy walked door-to-door in the black community. They helped other men, women, and young people pass out the leaflets.

For two days the boycott had been more or less a secret. Very few white people in Montgomery knew about it. But on Sunday morning, all that changed. A story on the front page of the Montgomery *Advertiser* told about the boycott. Mr. Azbell had written a story using Mr. Nixon's information. He'd also used information from Mrs. Robinson's and Dr. King's leaflets.

Some whites were angry and upset. The chief of police went on television. He angrily spoke against the boycott. "Negro goon squads are scaring blacks from riding the buses," he falsely charged. "The police will help anyone who wants to ride the buses," he announced.

"I figure the niggers will just get right back into them buses like they always done," another white said. "They'll move right to them back seats like always." Like some other whites, this person didn't think black people would stand up for their rights.

Black churches were full of joyful singing, preaching, and praying on Sunday morning. The ministers reminded church members to stay off the buses on Monday.

But some blacks were still not sure about the boycott. Some of them were afraid their white bosses would fire them. They knew their bosses could find almost any reason to let them go. Causing trouble over segregation was as good a reason as any. Some blacks were also afraid that the boycott might lead to bloodshed and death. They were afraid of what some whites might do when the boycott started.

Would enough people stay off the buses to make the boycott a success? As the sun set Sunday evening, no one knew for sure.

4

◆◆◆

No Riders Today!

Dr. King's wife, Coretta, looked out the window early Monday morning. What she saw did not make her happy. It was a gray, cold, cloudy day. It wasn't the kind of day that would make people want to walk to work or stand around waiting for cars. She wondered whether people really would stay off the buses on a day like this.

Soon, Mrs. King saw the headlights of one of the buses. As the bus drew closer, she could see inside. She saw the driver—and no one else. She looked again to make sure. Then she shouted to Dr. King, who was in the kitchen, "Martin, Martin, come quickly!"

Dr. King raced to the window. Mrs. King pointed to the bus. She was excited and proud. "Darling, it's empty!" she said, her voice full of joy.

Dr. King was amazed. He knew this bus was usually full of black people on their way to work. But today it rumbled slowly by, as empty as could be.

Dr. King was still not sure the boycott was working, however. He wondered whether all the buses would be as empty. He and Mrs. King waited anxiously for the next bus.

Sure enough, 15 minutes later, another empty bus rolled by. And after that, another one, with just two white people on it.

Dr. King wanted to see more. He got into his car and drove around Montgomery. He passed bus after bus for over an hour. During the whole time, he saw no more than eight black people riding the buses. He noticed that not many whites were riding the buses, either. Some of them had stayed off to help the boycott.

Instead he saw black men, women, and children walking. He saw them riding in black-owned cars and taxis. He even saw some people riding mules and some riding in buggies pulled by horses.

Some people walked as much as 12 miles to and from work or school. And they walked proudly. They knew why they were walking. They were walking for their rights—for their self-respect.

At some bus stops, children laughed and made faces as the buses rolled by. They joked about the "yellow monsters" and sang out, "No riders today!" Some adults, too, pointed and laughed at the empty buses. "Who will you kick now?" they shouted to the drivers.

Dr. King and the other leaders were happy. The boycott was even more successful than they'd hoped it would be. Almost no one from the black community rode the buses. And almost no one from the black community shopped in the stores downtown. The buses and the businesses lost money. This showed the mayor that the black community

was strong. It showed the city and the bus drivers that they could not get away with treating blacks unfairly.

But there was still work to do. Monday afternoon, the community leaders met. They began to make plans for the big meeting that night. First, they voted on a new name for their group. They called themselves the Montgomery Improvement Association, or MIA, for short. Next, they elected Dr. King as the president of their group. Mr. Nixon was elected treasurer.

The new group decided that black people should not ride the buses again until certain changes were made. They made a list of the changes they wanted:

1. Drivers must be polite to black riders.
2. Black riders can take any seat, starting from the back and going forward. White riders can take any seat, starting from the front and going backward. Nobody has to get up to give another person a seat.

3. Black bus drivers should be hired for routes in the black neighborhoods.

Five thousand people came to Holt Street Baptist Church that night. People filled every corner of the church. Hundreds of people stood outside in the cold weather. Some stood on boxes and peeked through the windows.

At first the crowd was quiet and curious. They had never been part of a boycott before. They didn't know what was going to happen at the church. Many of them had never heard of Dr. King.

Soon, Dr. King began to speak. Loudspeakers carried his deep voice to the people outside the church. "We are here this evening—for serious business," he said slowly. A few people murmured "yes" as he paused before continuing. Dr. King could tell that most of the people in the crowd were holding back. They were waiting for him to fill them with a feeling of pride, hope, and courage about the boycott.

As he spoke, his powerful voice rang out. "We are here," he said, "because . . . we are American citizens." He reminded them of what had happened to Mrs. Parks. "Just the other day . . . one of the finest citizens in Montgomery . . . was taken from a bus—and carried to jail and arrested—because she refused to give up—to give up her seat to a white person."

Each time he paused, more and more people shouted "yes" and "Amen." They understood the unfairness of what had happened. They were angry, too. They agreed with Dr. King that Mrs. Parks was a brave and noble woman. "And just because she refused to get up, she was arrested," he repeated. There were more shouts and a few people clapped.

After they quieted down, he went on. His voice was even stronger now. His eyes blazed as he looked at the crowd, and sweat began to show on his brow. "And you know, my friends," he said, "there comes a time when

people get tired of being trampled over by the iron feet of oppression."

The crowd exploded with a chorus of "yes." They were with him now. The strong voice and carefully chosen words of Dr. King had filled them with the pride of being citizens who had a right to be treated better. They listened and then answered his words with clapping and shouting. He asked them to work together and stand up for their rights.

When he finished, everyone clapped and shouted wildly. He had made an important speech that they would remember for a long time.

Finally, Mr. Abernathy asked everyone if they wanted to end the boycott. "No!" roared the crowd. One strong voice proudly shouted out what everyone was thinking, "This is just the beginning!" And everyone clapped and yelled in loud agreement.

Epilogue

Indeed, it was only the beginning. White officials refused to change the bus-segregation law. Bus drivers refused to be polite. Instead, the officials tried to force blacks to ride the buses again. They declared the boycott illegal. Black leaders, including Dr. King, Mrs. Robinson, and Mr. Nixon, were arrested.

Then a few whites became violent. They ruined Mrs. Robinson's new car by throwing acid on it. They bombed the homes of Dr. King, Mr. Abernathy, and Mr. Nixon.

But the black community stuck together. They did not become violent in return. They

kept walking. They kept riding in their own cars and taxis. They believed in the boycott because they believed in their rights. They believed they deserved to be treated fairly. This belief gave them the courage to keep walking.

Some people walked even when they were offered rides. One grandmother shook her head and said "No thanks" when someone offered her a ride. "I'm walking for my children and my grandchildren," she said proudly. Black people stayed off the Montgomery buses.

From around the world, people sent money to help the Montgomery Improvement Association. The money helped pay the bail bonds for leaders who were arrested. That way the leaders did not have to stay in jail.

The money also helped pay someone to keep the cars and taxis on schedule, just like the buses, planes, and trains. That way, people were able to get where they had to be on time.

Finally, on November 13, 1956, the boy-cotters won a great victory. The Supreme Court agreed with three judges who had ruled that the Montgomery bus-segregation law was not legal. The ruling became official on December 20. It stated that black people must be allowed to sit anywhere they chose— front or back. Thirteen months after it began, the boycott was finally over.

Black citizens of Montgomery were relieved. They were glad that the law was finally on their side. They were glad the boy-cott had worked. But there was no big cele-bration.

"I don't recall that I felt anything great about it," said Mrs. Parks many years later. "It didn't feel like a victory, really," she said.

Many people remembered the bitter events of the past year. They had fought a long, hard battle, and now it was over. Perhaps they were sad that they had to fight it at all. Perhaps they knew that many more battles remained to be fought. The boycott

had been the first big blow to segregation. But many more such blows were needed before segregation would be defeated. It was a good beginning, but it was just a beginning.

Early on December 21, Dr. King, Mr. and Mrs. Abernathy, E. D. Nixon, and a white man, Glenn Smiley, got on a city bus.

As Dr. King paid his fare, the driver smiled. "I believe you are Reverend King, aren't you?" he asked.

"Yes, I am," Dr. King replied, smiling back.

"We are glad to have you this morning," said the driver.

"Thank you," said Dr. King, and he took a seat in the front of the bus.

Afterword

This story told how black people in the community of Montgomery, Alabama worked together to solve a problem. Some of the people in the community later wrote books about what happened. Those books were used in writing this story. Reporters wrote news stories about what happened. Their news stories were also used in writing this story.

Notes

Page 5 Laws that enforced segregation in the South were called Jim Crow laws. No one is sure where the name *Jim Crow* came from. But beginning in the 1890s, *Jim Crow* came to stand for any law or act that kept black people from doing the same things or going to the same places as whites. Black people had to sit in separate sections of movie theaters, parks, trains, waiting rooms, and restaurants, as well as buses. They could not use the same public restrooms or even drink from the same water fountains as whites.

Page 11 In Montgomery in 1955, there were 50,000 black people and 75,000 whites. About 40,000 black people rode the buses. Only 12,000 whites rode the buses.

Page 12 The idea of black riders boycotting the buses was not new. As early as 1900, blacks in 27 cities had boycotted streetcar lines. Blacks in Baton Rouge, Louisiana, had boycotted city buses twice in 1953. After the second boycott, only two seats in the front of each bus were "for whites only." One row of seats in the back was "for blacks only." Black and white people could sit in the other seats on a first-come, first-served basis.

Page 16 Mr. Nixon had been the president of the Montgomery NAACP (National Association for the Advancement of Colored People) from 1947 to 1951. He was president of the Alabama NAACP until 1952. He, too, like Mrs. Robinson, helped many black people register to vote.

Page 28 Mrs. Robinson was already a member of Dr. King's church, Dexter Avenue Baptist Church. She was on the Political Action Committee, helping people register to vote. She also worked for the NAACP.

Pages 33–37 The aim of the boycott was to show the power of the black community. Dr. King said, "We were withdrawing our cooperation from an evil system rather than merely withdrawing our economic support from the bus company." The bus company lost more than $750,000 during the boycott.

Page 37 Mrs. Robinson was an active member of several MIA committees. She became the editor of the MIA newsletter and drove her car in the car pool, mornings and afternoons, after teaching at the college. Dr. King said she was more active "on every level of the protest" than any other person.

Pages 37–38 A group of people from the MIA met with the mayor and a lawyer for the bus company. Not much came of this meeting. The lawyer was opposed to the changes the MIA members wanted. "If we granted the Negroes these demands," the lawyer said, "they would go about boasting of a victory they had won over the white people; and this we will not stand for."

Page 42 Members of the MIA had a second meeting with the mayor and white citizens on December 17, 1955. At this meeting, the mayor formed a committee of eight white people and five black people. The mayor wanted this committee to come up with a way to solve the boycott crisis. Mrs. Robinson was quick to point out to the mayor that the committee should have the same number of blacks as whites. The mayor reluctantly agreed.

Pages 42–44 The black ministers gave people lessons in nonviolence. They would line up chairs like those on a bus. They would ask a few people to sit in the chairs. Then they would have some other people play white passengers and bus drivers. The "white" players would taunt or provoke the black passengers. The ministers helped the people learn how not to show their anger and remain peaceful.

Page 45 The Montgomery bus company was actually owned by National City Lines, Inc., a company in Chicago. That company owned buses in 35 cities throughout the United States. After the Supreme Court ruling, the company made an announcement. It told its Montgomery drivers it was not going to disobey the court's orders. It said any driver who didn't want to obey the orders should quit. Six out of one hundred drivers did.

Richard Kelso lives and works in New York City where he is a staff writer for Curriculum Concepts. Mr. Kelso has also written *Days of Courage* and *Building a Dream* for the *Stories of America*.